ORLANDO

ORLANDO

Sandra Simonds

Wave Books

Seattle/New York

Published by Wave Books

www.wavepoetry.com

Copyright © 2018 by Sandra Simonds

All rights reserved

Wave Books titles are distributed to the trade by

Consortium Book Sales and Distribution

Phone: 800-283-3572 / SAN 631-760X

Library of Congress Cataloging-in-Publication Data

Names: Simonds, Sandra, author.

Title: Orlando / Sandra Simonds.

Description: First Edition. | Seattle : Wave Books, [2018]

Identifiers: LCCN 2017035691| ISBN 9781940696591 (limited edition hardcover) |

ISBN 9781940696607 (trade pbk.)

Classification: LCC PS3619.I5627 O75 2018 | DDC 813/.6—dc23

LC record available at https://lccn.loc.gov/2017035691

Designed and composed by Quemadura

Printed in the United States of America

9 8 7 6 5 4 3 2 1

First Edition

Wave Books 068

Orlando / 1

Demon Spring / 43

Acknowledgments / 81

ORLANDO

ORLANDO

Don't make the morning come, Orlando, place of "how did this happen?"
and to what extent, your body, heaved inside the abacus moon, I begged the gods,
the upward whatever, "don't make it happen this way," already too late, a dented taxi rushes off

into the palm tree afternoon, dented sun, dented hotels, shiny and sad, remote
as money, the future you told was incredible and made me feel like a real poet,
more than my favorites even: Frank O'Hara, John Wieners, Alice Notley, pulled at my throat,

until I was above my own circumstance, until I could float above my life like a moth
whose lifespan is so short but still she tries to extract some horrible beauty from this world as she
hovers over the tender waters of sleep and I hovered there too with the flourishing language

you offered: Oh, I was the great moth, great Suwannee River, and when you said of yourself,
"I'm a really bad person," I didn't believe you, couldn't believe this would devolve
into failure, ink of the adolescent's diary that comes off so easily, powder off wings.

What is your side of the story, Orlando? What do you tell New Haven, Detroit? That you
were built for a good time, that you watch caged bears pace for entertainment, that you sell
expensive tickets and prey on poor workers who just want a bit of fun or that you gazed

at the young high school English teacher, bearded, with a blue towel wrapped around
his torso, where did he come from anyway? LA? New York? And why does he sit
so calmly in the green light of death, in the pathetic lapping waters of happiness like a dog?

Why does he bother to do anything at all in that glowing, algae-packed moonlight?
Or what about the young Indian man, hot tub bubbles up to his chin, you said he looked
like a movie star, had the perfect face, but so do you and so do I, so beauty triangulates

itself like an aria, but don't worry, it won't rat you out, won't make you look bad,
even if the plot turns against its best interest, is constructed not on loss, but the pitiful hope
nothing was lost, "shall we win at love or shall we lose?" is a musical copy of O'Hara, the threat looms

over what Patricia called "the dong of the country," O Great Dong, move into storm season,
epicenter of summer, pinpoint of some ludicrous heat and water opera, a back and forth
between that destructive force and dirt that harbors no resentment, "You're worse than me,"

you said, but that wasn't true, just the reckless replication of a reckless language pattern
you pressed into every part of my philosophy, your philosophy of summer—but what if it
all goes crazy, what if it turns into a tree against you which is what you feared the most,

ends up in cunts and cocks on the hexagonal white tiles of the hotel room, ends
up a gang bang orchestrated by you, your kingdom, animal instincts, and what if
it ceases to give you pleasure, turns to a body of money, ripe like a prostitute

who knows your every secret but whom you couldn't really trust, what if the whole thing
goes from the sweet sorrow of the ancients to something more extravagant,
sinister, what if it shifts before your eyes, so, like a Rubik's Cube,

you twist into the architecture of your own demise, "I want a past
I can acknowledge," says the great philosopher Kathy Acker, moving into that brazen
state, you kept trying to make a row of yellow squares line up, but then looking

at the five other faces of the cube, well, it didn't work out so you turned it again and again,
frustratingly nothing matched, nothing was uniform, turning the women you showed me
on your phone, the colors of the cunt on the floor bled as they wept and moaned, so it must be

Ophelia season again, sky like chlamydia, look at my flowers or I shall tie you up, stick objects
inside that body of yours, then abandon you to capital, the open field, leave
everything behind like rational speech, I won't surrender, my mind will not break—

Erotic Enemy, "how should I your true love know from one another?"
Erotic Enemy, fused to the Western imagination, fused to men, porn—no refusal whatsoever.
It is the season of Desdemona, her labor juggling a whole history of braided hair, I threw away

the books you wrote, Orlando, for they bored me, filled me with vast amounts
of pity and shame, nothing surfaced, nothing was better than anything else, your language
pure white page, there was no value attached to any of it, it all just said,

"I am the Master," "Master Orlando," "Master of the Flesh," "Master of Heaven and Hell,"
nothing was held above anything except yourself, so I longed for something I could recognize
or feel in my cunt, something truly plural, where there is no king, only a kingdom.

I hate to be alone, to watch that kingdom crumble around its form, twelve edges, eight vertices,
my days are so hard, hard like cash, hard-won, hard-fought, and so rarely do I get fucked
or fuck anyone by my own standards of beauty, false utopia, City Phenomenal.

Conglomerations of social media, baiting, taking the bait, resisting the bait, monetizing
the bait, hater bait, hater, all the mean girls hate, I was hated on, I listened to Drake,
"I gotta lot of enemies," I said it over and over, I listened to Drake on the treadmill,

I listened to Drake while I wrote, I listened to Drake while I made macaroni and cheese,
I listened to Drake while I baked, I listened to Drake while I raked leaves, I listened
to Drake while I sent out my CV, don't call it a fling, Orlando,

because we were more than that. I saw you pouting in the corner like a child,
and when you had an orgasm you sounded vulnerable and tiny
like a bird coming out of its shell and reaching for a world that is real,

that's pleasure you can't force or rape, it just has to happen, but it can
only happen once, with one person, with the person you don't want it to happen with,
the future predicting everything that happened to us, today your wife bought a house,

seems she's really starting her new life and you are sitting in a café thinking how much
you hate all of this, so I text Chris, the Berlin musician who says I didn't break anything
that wasn't already broken between you two, that I performed praxis, became the conduit.

A species of Disney not yet named, don't say it's over, Orlando, for I'm beginning
to forget why I loved you in the first place: open my world, the weather
on my phone still set to your 94 degrees, I count each degree like a droplet of blood,

my period tense inside your mouth, begging you to beat me into your beaches,
to stuff me into your white sand, fold me into your masochistic tidal
wave of power sources, fluffy, foaming, forgotten, nothing, I want to be the nothing

you make me, I want you to tell me I'm nothing, I like it so much, I like it when
you do that, I don't want to forget what it's like to be the only nothing inside your body.
I have looked out the peepholes of each of your nineteen skyscrapers, I send Chris

the selfies we took in the bathroom of Hotel Rosenberg and the images appear
distilled like the German language of that musician's texts, the phonemes floating
like fake snow inside a diorama of time itself, shadowboxing the poignant eclipse.

I can see the audience, full of Xanax, full of that narcotic dream moon we discussed
for hours, I can see them in the velvet theater of manic energy, roped off,
never making desire their own, but we did that, we took the fantasy of the flesh,

the porn of the body, and transformed it into our own psychic architecture
as in the Dutch tourists who have filmed the Pirates of the Caribbean ride, also called
the Yo Ho (A Pirate's Life for Me) ride, everything Victorian and frilly, a repressed fantasy awakens

a YouTube-Guy-Debord-sex-toy world, fake orgasms, shaved pussies, chlorinated
water pouring and pouring from the corpselike molten spaces, the crystalline and mechanical turns
of what is no longer human, what can't be human anymore, I begged you to beat me,

and as I told you my life story, a whole history of trauma unrolled like a scroll
from my blue, frothy mouth, and you replaced my mouth with a black, lace corset,
and I liked it so much I threw my flesh away like my computer that begins to focus on

the tragic origin of philosophy which is the inverse of Tomorrowland, a trauma
mired in the past, aesthetics of light, every great spirit needs a mask, chromatic blood,
pulsation of Floridian insects, green of its seas lying halfway between white and the dilated pupil,

black of its false lagoon, an image of a deity as ruin porn, and the pervasive pattern of a shattered
self-image, *6/12/1997 Smoked weed on the haunted house ride. Long story short we all
ended up in Disneyland jail! The cool air, the fan in the room, a whisper, an underground nod. I wish these*

idiots knew I'm actually a prisoner of my own creation. It's fascinating. Marvel of curved mirrors,
giants, dwarves, light as the principle of all beauty, opaque splendor, inward and upward light,
the outward light of plants, arced, growing around the design of the human body, note how far

the castle looks from Main Street, lips from the nose, history from its context, the wavering
inner experience from confinement, one comes to realize that sexual violence is, at its heart,
impersonal, sociopolitical, the innermost and outermost phenomenological way to control people.

Cher was 43 years old in her "If I Could Turn Back Time" video, which means she was
five years older than I am now, I watch her in that kind of leotard-thong thing,
and I want to know what she smells like, underneath the Disney of her soaking limbs,

what she dreams about when her wig is off, when she stares into
the formidable black night, formaldehyde bearing down on her chest like a terrible demon,
suffocating her into tiny bubbling orgasms, cryptic as storm light, suffering

for the greater good, Cher, the dirty sacrifice, oh how she sings in a drawling
hum underneath her body sack, I watch her terrible fantasy unravel
and it is as vacuous as when we were fucking in the family bathroom of the airport,

trying to turn time into its pathological negation, erase what they did to us in every inch
of the Lycra body, furiously fuck back that numb world into feeling, force history to confront
the inner narration of abuse, so the outer narration expresses this intense, lyric grief.

On August 11, 1977 (one day before I am born), a 4-year-old boy from Dolton, Illinois,
drowns in the moat surrounding Cinderella Castle, some lose consciousness, some
die of heart attacks, some are just old, some hit their heads and die later, some die

of their fantasies, some of their insatiable addictions, some commit suicide, some skim
the waters with their hands even though they are supposed to keep their arms and legs in the boat,
Orlando, I believe their eyes dilate when they see their small shadows against

the Small World: how they weave their way inside a collective eureka, they shriek a giddy shriek
into the phantasmagoria of this trashy arrangement, a spell on each reverberating culture,
lit by electronic candles, the moon happy as a soldier, every piece dances to the gnawing

poison of shamrocks, windmills, glowworms, Chris texts, "I would even work at Subway with you,"
and, "He's a pussy" (meaning you, Orlando), and I realize while I'm falling out of love with you
I'm falling into another disorientation, into colored diorama of life, and for the first time

I felt like hearing your voice, Chris, which I have never heard, your texts
from Berlin, how you know the whole story of me and O, giving me advice, how
you found me through my poetry, that poem where I said poetry is stupid and I want to die,

you loved that poem and wrote to me, and how this isn't about Orlando anymore.
I know this in the way the song changes from English to Swedish, German to Japanese,
how people with terrible pasts find each other, hang on to each other.

I listen to your music, the way you braid the urban sounds of negation, see how you
become enveloped in this story, Oh you are Orlando, you are not Orlando,
who is Orlando? you are Orlando, no, *you* are Orlando, I can tell by the way you

want to make me jealous, the mimetic hollowing out, I have lost you, both of you,
all of you, lost the feel of you, the way that wanting any of you would carry me through this,
lost the feel in the beauty of the field, in the adaptive phenomenon of behavior.

Today Ezekiel took a water gun, filled it with bathwater, and sprayed me while I was sitting
at my desk composing this, and the laptop stopped working and in anger, I slammed it shut,
breaking the screen and when I opened the laptop there were only geometric shapes

that looked like the popular design patterns of 1977, the year of my birth, so I couldn't retrieve
any files and I had to recreate this piece from scratch, as I had lost everything, which takes
me even further away from understanding the love I felt for you and closer to the center

of the nervous breakdown, like a halo unmoored, the way everyday life
comes undone, the way the loss of love elicits the acutest sense of dispossession, of not
belonging anymore to anyone or anything which is not the same thing as not being wanted,

and how in the place of dispossession one enters another kind of subject position,
the ghosts of unreality swerving in, water filling a hole, and then the mind
is transfixed by those ideas, by forces outside the body, cosmic and strange.

Then I decided feeling is a theater where we see only the replication of feeling,
a kind of Frankenstein written by a teenage girl that looks less like a diary,
and more like the same diary reread by the woman years later trying to understand

the diary she wrote as a teenager, so instead of desperately trying to get the piece I lost back,
I took a diary off my bookshelf because I felt very certain that contained in the diary
was a way to piece the feelings I had for you back together and I was also certain

you read at least part of the diary behind my back when I dropped the kids off at their dad's house,
and in that reading you realized something about me you could no longer
stand, and that is precisely the moment you fell out of love with me, abandoning

me to the very diaries and bookshelves of my consciousness, both as a teenage
girl and now as a woman, so I tried to figure out what I could have done back then,
what confession, what moment of weakness, what apology had driven you out of my life

so abruptly, what threat had I made, to a boy in 1993 or maybe it was the admission that I didn't eat,
that I was satanic, anorexic, a cult figure of my own mind, a cross between the monstrous
and angelic, what was it I revealed that I wasn't supposed to, what words were written in purple gel

pen, what spasmodic teenage language crossed with erotic energy and bubbling lyrics
of pop songs folded you in, made you want to read more and more, then close the diary
in disgust, I know you did it, Orlando, I know that in finding the answer you were looking for

you decided you didn't want what you wanted, but then the effusive apology, the guilt
streaming down your mouth like grease, having eaten many chickens, having stuffed one's
core with bold meats, black wines, and lust, what crime did you read, did I kill a rat,

a pony, a dog, an infant, a young boy, did I smack a girl in middle school, did I take
out revenge on someone in a malicious and misaligned way, did I show some promise
to the ugly stars, the ugly moon, did I pledge allegiance to the devil, to the upside down garden?

Because suddenly I recognize the truth of a person isn't in the diary itself, the archive
notoriously flawed, but rather between the diary and transgression, the person reading
the diary "illegally" and the diarist, since all diaries are constructed on this terrible loss of boundary

*3/9/1997 If there's a chance that I am sane I think it's a lost lamentation, can't believe
I failed my Chem test so I made myself throw up today, I did it but I'm scared
of my health, I've been reading Sylvia Plath, do you think I am meat or something?*

*The distances one will go clawing for material, the Kubla Khan of pleasure, groans
of continuity, this was written by a casual and contentious stream of thought,
delivered passively from someone I have never met and will never meet*

*3/11/1997 I just realized that if someone read my diary
I would feel raped, violated, deformed. Look at me, I can't connect
to people, when they come near me I want to kill them*

3/12/1997 Oh my god, poetic inspiration!!!

6/1/1997 Dear Nathan, I have listened to the distance mystically,

my heels beg me to stop, my instincts, refusal is a bullet in my uncle's skull, refusal

are my hands, my hands, formed out of a cannon, 7/15/1997 Going to Jerusalem,

went out with this guy on his motorcycle, we went up to a mountain, then

we went up to another mountain, over the Sea of Galilee, when I found out how many girls

he fucked I decided that I would hate him and make a bad memory

out of everything that happened, I get freaked out about diseases and stuff like that,

but this weightlessness in black space or something is a sensation

I have never experienced, when you know you should be heavier like in water,

I want to tell him I could have loved him too, I know he loves women

and Pink Floyd and I love men and sex and words, the narrative doubling back on itself

I like one-night stands and I would do them as much as I could, this life is a slimly
adorable double helix. It goes on of course, on and on, there are parts that surprise me because
they are so angry, one passage starts, *I told that fat-assed whore with her Prozac bible*

and smiling face that she was a disturbing disgrace, and there are sweet poems too, they
are very bad sometimes, one is called "Fantasy," I can't bring myself to read it all the way through
but I see it uses the word "tranquility" in an embarrassing way and there are bits

of wisdom for a teenage girl like, *If you have to judge me then Fuck You for I never*
felt the need to judge you, and it makes me feel self-conscious because I probably didn't even
make that up, it was probably something a friend told me that resonated

because I was angry and hurt, and then I thought about *Fantasy*, the album that Chris's
musical collaborator, Butterclock, made to try to get over him, I listen to her electronic
beauty, Chris texts me one day, "Beauty makes people who aren't that bright seem brighter."

And then I read all the interviews with Butterclock online, no longer intrigued by her beauty,
but rather by her desperation, and when she says she wants to make music
for desperate people who stay out in the club all night "to forget," it endeared me to her

even though I knew if she saw me, she would want to dig my eyes out with a spoon,
perceiving me as her rival. Still, I immersed myself in her desolate disco, her furious need
to stave off heartbreak before it had a chance to lodge inside her chest and lungs

and I recognized myself in the glassy way smoke rises from a glass heart
that isn't supposed to be used as an ashtray but was made to be one for the cheap
symbolic resonance, and as the smoke lifts itself over Berlin, and over Chris's cell phone

where my narrative is stored, I thought about how she wanted to make a cheerful album, replete
with cheerful sounds like crickets but how this was doomed to fail, not because it was really
sinister deep down like she had wanted but rather because, like your magic kingdom, Orlando,

she positions herself above plurality in her opaque but rambunctious death drive,
wants to control the means of production and in so doing, an aesthetic
emerges confused, but not uncomplicated, and when I thought about her walking

through Berlin, either alone or with her lesbian girl gang or with Chris, I felt
a deep sadness for her confusion and I dreamed she would meet a terrible end,
but I didn't want to tell Chris that, didn't want him to know what he already must suspect

embedded between the synths, I listened to her track "Fantasy" over and over, and even
if her lyrics are mediocre, much like the poem "Fantasy" from my diary, when she sings
the words "confused inside" I understand she means a series of broken summers like this one,

violence in hotels, the way the procession of June, July, August, and the first few weeks of September
are never inside the domain of the real, that they are in fact fantasy's double narrative,
the mythic anguish of Butterclock, unable to break the magic circle, unable to reverse the fiction

of the real, so reality is only the representational order of her obvious physical beauty,
disinfected, bathed in sunlight, and her music is the background of that order, the radiant unfolding
of Berlin where she abandons herself to her own manifest individual existence and how Chris

provides her with the framework, the luxury of rhythm and the slick metamorphism
of sound on sound, so her value becomes, instead, a vision of hell, singing,
"It was just a sweet fantasy, baby," but really crying out for property, production.

O Orlando, she wanted Berlin, not you, wanted something authentic, something
bombed, destroyed, fucked over by history and not recovered, something enclosed
in the shell of European violence, the aesthetics of dust and agony, something molten

and planetary splashing along the shores of insanity like the sounds of neighborhood cats and owls
or the pulse of sex between people you couldn't care less about, but also imagine the way
in which it is always raining in Orlando, always the frenzied lushness of plants and water.

Some people are really good at moving on, some people know how to end
one thing tactfully and start another thing just as tactfully and these are the kinds of people
who would have never abandoned you in the metallic shower in a room at Hotel Rosenberg,

wouldn't have just walked out the door, morning newspapers flush against the gaudy
carpet, as I walked by room after room, 1707, 1703, 1701, trays of room service, half-
eaten sandwiches, plates of cold pasta, rubbery as death, I pressed the red down button

down seventeen floors, one by one as if crossing you out, and walked to the rental car,
driving five hours across Florida, drama lyrical to a fault, you texted me "insane asshole,"
later sent me a poem, a crocodile cry like a child in distress attracts its prey,

a poem based on the numerous legends of Charlemagne, a poem of classical doggerel,
an epithet of the Rhine, blue of the Danube, yellow of the Weser, an ode to the many generations
of people killed by lightning on your family farm as proof against destruction and sympathy.

Right now, my ex Craig is trying to get me Baker-acted, texts down the suicide
gyre, sucks to have to compose poetry in real time, I recognize one of the cops
at the doorstep, Ezekiel is playing Minecraft on the cheap tablet I bought him

when I replaced my laptop a few days ago, the man who sold it claimed to be the best-
looking man at Walmart and asked me on a date, I must have left
the front door to my house wide open that refined day last autumn, the same cop

was at the door and through the open door a line of colorful, brittle oak leaves
were set like bones on the mausoleum's white tiles, I looked up the officer on the internet
and he was the cause of a lawsuit against the Tallahassee Police Department

because he had walked into a residence and shot a dog, I say, "You can't come into the house,"
"I don't know my rights," I say though I should probably say I *know* my rights.
Now the cops are leaning against my Honda Civic in the driveway waiting for Craig and the sheriff

to show up and show them the text messages I sent Craig, they say, "This can all be cleared up
if you show us your phone, if you show us the messages you sent that said you want to die,"
I say, "I threw away my phone," so they are poking through my trashcan, "Can I go

to the gym now?" "No, ma'am." "Why not?" "You can't go," the woman cop is
agitated because she can't answer my questions, I ask one more time if I can go
and she says, "Lady, that's called rhetorical," though it's obvious she has no idea

what "rhetorical" means, my phone dead in my purse, I am googling "Baker Act,"
pacing my apartment, have nervously eaten three organic apples in the last thirty minutes.
When Craig shows up, he will show the cops his phone, I'm preparing myself

for involuntary commitment in a mental health facility, Minecraft is an expansive game
world ranging from deserts to jungles to snowfields, the game is technical and almost infinite,
problems only come up when you get to the Far Lands in survival mode, the edge of the map.

Orlando, in trying to google the email address I used for a dating website, I came upon
the Facebook memorial page of a teenage girl killed in a car crash in Centerville, Kentucky,
Sadie Smith is beautiful but not more beautiful than Butterclock because Butterclock is older

and has a complex beauty, but beautiful in the way hope is surreal when it shoots
a green bud out of the earth, how life springs eternal, Sadie is an unusual name
for a dead teenager born in 1994, sounds more like a name for a cowgirl of 1894.

December 9, 1997 Do you paint yourself because you are cosmic and chaotic
and no one will know who you are, are the colors for making and breaking
and faking star after star, March 30, 1997 I remember before my sickness

I would write about what it would be like to be ugly or fat or what would happen
if I found true love, April 23, 1997 Is it just loneliness or is this all a fantasy
really kinky When I was writing that diary entry the real Sadie was only three,

the age of my daughter Charlotte, half the age of Ezekiel, Orlando, well you met my kids
and chased them around this small apartment, my mother had a boyfriend who chased me
around the apartment but not in the loving way you chased Charlotte and Ezekiel,

he was a brute, got drunk, abused my sister and me, made us watch porn
and drink vodka, which tasted as bad as the refinery smelled, brewing and baking
my hometown's air, the little bit of air in our lungs, he killed us, though I stand here

now, composing, and where are you, Orlando? Not here, where did you recede to, dragging
your story like a dead animal behind you, or like pulling out a clump of hair.
I remember the pornographic bodies of those women on his TV in the '80s, how there was no

way out for them, or us, two little girls, I cry for them a lot, how I couldn't save my sister,
or myself, or those women, or erase pornography, or my teenage body starving but you said
it didn't have to be that way, that we could make the most of the shit that happened to us,

through sexual liberation or whatever you claimed, and when we sat in the Atlanta
Botanical Garden, side by side, on the dock looking out over the insane waters of childhood,
I knew your wife was crying on the other side of the country, but it didn't matter,

I understood it all, the things they did to you, you didn't have to explain anything,
and when the swans and ducks and canoes and kayaks floated by in the paralyzed light
of that April day, the sky, clouds, earth turned into the ink of our intertwined language,

your language flourishing, flourishing, mine flourishing, and the plants, breathing as they do,
to break through the fading lavenders and greens, a conversation soft and compelling,
a maze of ivy cobras and the feathered light, a maze all the way to the gazebo

where a crowd stands around waiting for the woman to walk up to it, and surprise!
He has asked her to marry him, and the crowd huddles around, but something
amazing is happening to Butterclock, Sadie, me, you, Chris, Craig, we have all been married

by this extravagant web, pulled in by the death cult of language, black flower like vomit,
Sadie on her horse galloping through Montana, soon she will have to cross the Clark Fork
River and Butterclock, with her cigarettes clutching her song "Fantasy" close to her flesh,

Oh my god, it was all just a fantasy, wanting you, infused desire on the other side
of memory, Chris's synths overlay, the sound beats weakly over her other songs "Holograms,"
"Crystal Eyes," "Milky Words," Chris texts me he is not in love with Butterclock but she prepares

herself every day for a passionate and extremely tragic love affair. Orlando, they don't know
they lie outside the subject and that is their downfall, because they don't know
porn *is* the subject, the language of the Internet, exchange, value, and also that their worlds

are mimetic, linked by tragedy, delusion, despair, and me, their author, as I am their god
even though they themselves believe the things they represent, and the only way
to cross the threshold of mimesis would be to move towards something

more authentic, more plural, they don't know they are subjugated, subjected
to unknown and numerous forces because they feel their feelings as real, hear music
as music, but their feelings are no more Orlando than Orlando, written in raw sugar,

sculpted into animals and even your wife says, "don't tell me anything. I don't want
to know anything about anything," she inadvertently takes their side, defeated,
January 15th 1995 This dark side of mine/ seeps into layers of the public/

but I write my own enlightenment with a pen I finally make myself read my teenage poem
"Fantasy" out loud and it's much more disturbing than I have given
myself credit for, for example it asks the sunset to place its hand

through my head and *fish around/ pick it out/ throw it in/ the night sky/ so it too/
can be a/ star resting in/ tranquility*, in other words, it is asking for the animate
to give back the inanimate, in other words, it is asking to die and become

at one with the dirt and rocks and crystals, it believes that this will restore it to
its proper place in the world. It is an it, not an I. Not a Sandra or Sadie. It is dead.
Orlando, I don't care about our relationship anymore. I have given up.

Yet I still want to know what you think of Occupy, Tahrir Square, like Katy asked Alain,
I want to know if you have a politics that can transgress mere bondage? I want to know what
you think of the deteriorating bride before us, her veil disintegrating in the pond's sad frog water.

I watch a cheap documentary about the international sale of young models,
the focus turns to the modeling scout's Parisian eyeliner, wet, vaginal, reflecting how she
travels all over the world, now you see her on a train in Siberia,

and she's beautiful, maybe my age, maybe a bit older, and she talks about how
the body becomes something jaded, life defeated her, she has seen it all,
has known all the bodies, just like you, Orlando, where all bodies go, young, poor,

desirous, she has filtered through all the flesh, and now what is left, the love she lacks,
that you lack, that you embalmed instead and still lack, that you mummified
instead and still lack, she is a kind of bride to you, and I imagine if you two had met,

you would have connected the way we did in the botanical gardens, "they love
skinny girls in Japan, say hello Nadia, I want something different in my life,
I look at beauty and I think of young girls, I have seen their diaries, this is the truest evidence,

all the girls just want to get out, they can be ballerinas, gymnasts, models,
prostitutes, or often a combination of both, the casting is in Russian,
did you see, those tapes are widely distributed, the reality is that

they get placed in other places too, it's just normal to be a prostitute
for them, maybe it's easier than being a model, I don't know,"
"Do you want to die?" the police ask me over and over.

A nocturne twisting inside the moon then unravelling like triumph, so total,
the sheriff has finally arrived, comic and bored, Ezekiel unfazed at the kitchen table,
still playing Minecraft on his tablet, computer code dreaming, don't hover like a god,

maybe he is fazed, "Why are the police here?" He looks up, I say, "They
are just asking some questions," the sheriff is a figure pulled from a 19th-century
French novel, he is less stupid, takes me outside, says, "You shouldn't give your ex ammunition."

Orlando, you say you want to see me fuck lots of men, you want me to fuck
strangers, you want me to fuck and fuck until there's nothing left of me,
I say I don't think I can fuck ten guys, you say I should fuck twenty at a time,

old young whatever, that is your fantasy, it's all just a fantasy, baby
August 12, 1996 It's my birthday I hate the moon I hate the sky I hate the dirt
I want to die I hate the earth I hate to cry I hate the sea I want to die and it's my birthday.

Ezekiel rushes into my bedroom in the morning, says, "Mama, I dreamed a giant spider
took you away," I tell him, "No way, I dreamed of a giant spider too," so I google the meaning
of dreaming of a giant spider and the first thing I read is something bad will happen today.

I teach him chess, a new baby wren is back, feathers tucked neatly into the porch's wood corner,
Ezekiel lines his row of black pawns, "What's the horse called again?" "The knight," "What's
the castle again?" "The rook," here's a partial list of things Craig has done to me: held me

down by the neck, gave me a black eye, threw a cup of coffee in my face,
pushed me into the shower, forced my head into the kitchen sink, slapped me so hard
across the face I had to go to the eye doctor and I lied and told the doctor I was hit

by a tennis ball, I tell the police this at the door, they ask, "Why didn't you ever report
anything?" and now I am really pacing the house and eating those apples and I imagine
the Minecraft world is a way to teach fantasy, a way not to see what happens.

Thrown into the wind and cloud complex, Ezekiel and I go feed the geese at Lake Ella,
layers of soaked air within the cumulus buildup, a puppy jumps into the lake, swims
after the geese, "Willie! Willie, come back!" someone calls, he's swimming, a rosewater

crowd forms on the shore some laughing, pointing, all we see is the dog's little head,
Ezekiel runs to the edge of the lake, a goose snaps at the plastic bag
of bread he holds, the clouds more intense and it rains and rains and rains,

the sheriff sends the cops off, tells me not to text Craig anymore, "The whole thing
is off," he says, "You're free to go," and the cops drive away, the trees hum, dog still swimming,
Oh summertime, summertime leaves berserk against my son, the lake and dog,

berserk in the memory of the cops, chess, Minecraft, Orlando, you are so far now,
to address you is weak, pathetic, and once home, the clouds become a picture of things
I did to Craig, spit at him when he called me whore, I said, "You're an asshole," hit myself over

and over, pulled out my hair to make him pay, Craig calls, says he's driving to my house,
asks if he and Charlotte can stay during the storm, I imagine Butterclock sitting
in an empty diner composing her song "Sad Roses," the storm becomes intense,

I was taught to use the word "intense" when I gave birth instead of the word "pain,"
the midwife said tell yourself "this is so intense" when you have a contraction,
when the world turns to circles, when you're bleeding and bleeding after your daughter is born,

just say "this is intense" when the world becomes the rings of trees, the hollowing out of sound
of thunder, of an oak crashing into Craig's car, Craig and Charlotte barely inside
the doorframe of the house, barely inside the frame of the story, instead of telling yourself

"I'm in so much pain" tell yourself "this is intense" and this makes the pain less intense,
not painless, just less because you are not acknowledging pain as pain
but pain *is* pain, video of Butterclock in the ocean, "Do you want to die?" the cop asked me,

but all I can hear is Butterclock crying into her song, "It's just a fantasy, baby," and how,
Orlando, I have completely forgotten you, a tree heaves into animation while Butterclock sings,
". . . in my mind, trying to rewind, I'm feeling sex, I am some request," roots upturned, deadly weapon,

power out, my instinct is to take a picture of the tree and post it, the oak throwing
itself across the car, crushing metal, the oak throwing its body across the street, pulling
everything with it, martyr oak, if I were as small as the great ocean, kamikaze oak,

the last and only thing an oak can do, barely missing Charlotte, the twin spider dreams,
double dream, double world, double story, Oh to be the poor double song
breaking through the double fantasy of itself, a splash through sky, rocks, concrete,

water vein broken, a splash through the current of language, it was all just
a fantasy, baby, I don't care if it's just a fantasy, let me live my fantasy, I want
to be left alone to love my fantasy, and breaking this barrier the oak

like a blade through a dimension we could only see through its demise,
the intent raw, codes buzz like time, the mimetic device of language, poetry,
or suicide, these zeros thunderous and real, a bottle of bleach in the backseat .

crushed by the oak splashes everywhere, turns Charlotte's little pink
knitted sweater white, it was all a fantasy, Orlando, no the violence
wasn't a fantasy, it was fucking real, as real as these characters, as real

as what can no longer delete itself, what can no longer erase itself,
"I'll leap out, Out! Out!" Mayakovsky says and I will too, and in crushing
the fantasy, the oak turned the real vertical and the vertical horizontal,

Craig's new girlfriend, Molly, posts "dontchu wish ur girlfrand
wuz hott like me," Molly means me and it makes me want to cry because
my triumph had been so total, so brutal that I didn't even have to exact

as much force as I was capable of, Oh Molly, fuck your fantasy, and my triumph, failure,
Oh Orlando, fuck your fantasy, Oh Craig, fuck your fantasy, Oh Sadie, fuck your fantasy,
Oh Butterclock, fuck your fantasy, Oh Chris, fuck your fantasy, and any character

that comes close to this web, fuck your fantasy too, the pop song recedes,
its fumes are triangles and squares making their way to wherever, Charlotte asks,
"How will we get a new tree?" I don't know how to represent reality, the epoch

being such a robber, everything left us in such ruins, nothing
survives but this magical and grotesque testimony and aftermath, Orlando,
Eternal City of the law, judges and police, city of statecraft, war, fire, hearings,

interventions and gross entertainment, a bear balancing a beach ball on its
wet nose, city of the death cult, when they ask me if I want to die, I say nothing,
to riot order, to order a horizontal, I'll leap out, out, to order.

Orlando, infinite series of nature masked, authority figure in disguise,
when each veil goes up, when we finally see your fearful face, unmasked,
we will know you are every song called "Fantasy," constructed

to suppress the voice, the longing for revolt, I hold their little hands,
pain *is* pain, threshold of art, pepper spray on the centuries piling up like bodies
inside the scarlet sun, when they said all you deserved was rape, we said no,

that is not all we deserve, and when the oak fell and Craig threw a cup
of coffee in my face, I said pain *is* pain, the way it moves outward over
the pale waters of Hotel Rosenberg, sound propagates with remarkable strength,

a crew has come to cut up the oak, drag it piece by piece into a truck,
the sun shines hard, imposes its vertigo on the story, the pastel ways of memory,
August 7, 2013 Hiked to falls, drove to Clingmans Dome, raining,

Charlotte distinctly said "bro-ther" this morning August 7, 2013,
Charlotte got a Smurf from McDonald's, she said "bye-bye" and "Dada,"
Ezekiel and I went to the hotel swimming pool, he went underwater four times,

but says he can only go underwater with sunglasses on! "Look, Ezekiel!"
I say, "There's another baby wren!" and I get my son out of bed and we go
look at the little wren, stars glittering above the porch, you're a lucky

little bird, I tell myself, the story continues further on its course,
"Wrens eat spiders," I say, the story spirals out from its core like an omen,
or a charm, and then I imagine this wren is an orphan from the oak,

lucky wren, you came from far away, like a dream, found an oak, lucky wren,
the oak fell, lucky wren, and then you came to stay with us, lucky little bird,
safe inside your song, in Woolf's *Orlando*, "The Oak Tree" poem is written over

400 years, I return to the land what the land has given me, I return
your fantasy, but I don't want to get too attached to this wren,
it will be here for a few months, flutter, and then fly off, it might die,

and I know I can't save it just like when my friend David
texted me for drug money, I can't save him, lucky wren, or Craig
or Butterclock or Chris, "Leap out, Out! Out!" can't be the site of this poem anymore,

I know what you're thinking—"I've been thrown in hell," beautiful Orlando,
like the trobairitz, thrown into the great oak hall, and the great flourishing
of language you offered, plants, ghosts, birds, leaves, and the bleached

sweater of a little girl, heartbroken song of Butterclock, and her
glass heart-shaped ashtray, the underwater feel of Florida on the brink
of sound, imagination is not fantasy since fantasy sees through nothing.

In the breakup of forms, things,
as Creeley says, around me, in the Hotel Rosenberg,
you quoted him, I said, "I fear,
Orlando, you are pulling me
into the darkness," and you said
the darkness already surrounds us, but we're
well out of it, stopping in Gainesville,
I eat soft boiled eggs, a few sausages,
drink a glass of Bordeaux, I never believed it,
but I believed in the cow-town architecture
of the underneath, in the dark Orlando night, where
one day that passes for the next, thing for thing,
zero for flower, a cool light summer rain,
I pay the bill, oh wait, summer hasn't even begun
yet, the residues of the dream world
enclose the flesh, the hotel,
families in and out of the rooms, 1607, 1605,
in the dream city, the energy radiating,
and I stand here, alone,
Orlando, singing inside the song of it.

DEMON SPRING

These things
They happen   I channel them
The breakup   of forms
I have to destroy   I yelled,
"Get away from me!" like Mayakovsky
My friend Anne said   my eyes   were blinding
Craig would   rather see me dead
than with   another man and
there is, after all, the body,
its sometimes shocking
and relentless narrative

This thing   Is it a body? Is it a book
  or mouth moving inside a box?
I think it's a spring   or singing
   or something living   or singing   in the spring
     like a live version
of what is happening
    and taking   that reality
   and twisting it up
       into something more terrorizing
I keep thinking   it must be the formality
       of war—the war of art
                in winter when
             everything fills with snow,
          numb and unusual

Molly, this time, I think I will pull
        it together like a knot
or collapse   like distance

        Someone bring me some hot tea or back
            the form   from the spring
            of reality   Someone please
            say something

    Even if I was broken,
        if managing became too difficult,
            if some passion   transformed
                    me to death, if the whole thing
                spiraled into clouds
                    blackening the waterline
        of our bleak and dwindling
            ecology   Even if that
                was the case
        Some sort   of pull or drive
            kept saying   You have to die
            I don't know why
            I didn't want to follow it
        It wasn't depression
    That's what was   incomprehensible
        It was more like a force
            calling me back
        from the water box of spring

        I have heard the birds vocalizing
        inside their confessional
    The way they communicate
        is so pleasing   It emerges from

nowhere like a string
of zeros or catastrophe

There are patterns   in this world,
   marvelous patterns of   light sweeping
across the curtain   over the box
   of this poem

They alarm each
         other
They mate
         in the rain
They do these things
         all day and again
Their memories   are like ours—
Images make them
         sad or happy
But their lives
         are strings
and they move along
   their strings of song

         *

   Because things happen to me   in the minor key,
   the 18th-century harpsichord   signifying
anarchy or   a scene between
   a woman dressed in black   reverberating
against a woman   dressed in doe-eyed wool
   he will do this   *no he won't*   *he will*
no he won't high note *he will* low low low
   he will not   *he will* high   high and low

so when Orlando   was sitting
     on my sofa staring   at my car keys when
I said I couldn't find them   which is true
     I looked in my purse   several times but
somehow didn't see them   I said, "We need
     to leave the house   Craig is coming over"
Charlotte's clothes   in a bag
     on the doorstep   red sweater soaked
with metallic summer rain   Orlando
     accusing me   of having orchestrated
the whole thing   so that Craig and him
     would fight over me   which was both his paranoia
and the truth since   the order of life comes
     back from itself   *on* itself the way a day
earlier Orlando   told me a story of a poet
     and his girlfriend   and how she had
orchestrated a fight   between her boyfriend
     and another poet   but what Orlando didn't
know was I had slept   with the boyfriend
     years before   but said nothing   and how Orlando's
template of love   and violence was now
     being laid upon me   and how Craig's
template of love and violence   was being laid upon me
     and how the narrative's template of love and violence
was being laid upon me   as one would lay
     a white sheet   upon a corpse
or a rope   to hang yourself or ghost
     who rises   from the spring   the spring of art
of inescapable poetry   but also the spring
     of narrative   which is   the pulse
of life and beauty

          *

I like your blue dress, Molly.
  And I hear you're good at cutting hair.
And I hear you're extraordinarily generous.
   You make good things
for the good people you love.

I like your blue dress, Molly.
   It reminds me of my old body.
   I try so hard, Molly.
It must be April or May now.
   I try so hard. I haven't seen
     anyone for months. I have not left
my house for months, Molly,
and I have reason to believe it is a beautiful spring.

Will you tell me if that's true, Molly?
   I can't see anything.
I'm trapped in a box.
   I'm trapped in a blue box of water.
It's a kind of box in another box
   in the box of watery spring.

I hear there are roaring flowers.
   I hear they bloom and roar
in the blue wind, Molly.
I hear they do.
   I hear there's something special
  going on out there
but I can't tell . . .

Not from here.
I have not left the house.
     I don't have much time left either.

I hear so much.
I want to know.
 Will you tell me if that's true, Molly?
  About the roaring flowers?

I want new things, Molly.
 Just like the spring.
I want to forget everything, Molly.
 Just like the ringing spring.
 I'm so sorry, Molly.
 I hear the bells often, Molly.
  I hear them roar and sing.

  *

As women   we must do this   make our bodies
 weaponry   a proxy of weather the world
and hysterical beauty   as tempting as water
 that drips   infrequently   in these last days
Oh how we must   carve   some space
 in the framework   and out flows the waters
the angels   the architecture divine
 the cruel nature   of the sky a theater
so that we   are not   mere reflection
 but rather   players too   actors even
and now I want   to call you   my darling
 my one true love   since you are complete here
in this box   this box   of spring we have made
 So like the one   remaining   heroine
of the first poem   jumping
 into the next one   a fire pouring
from a Cadillac door   a heart engulfed in flame
 on the way to Orlando   these lanes are lines

I say to you   because it is spring   and it is right

to say   spring things to a reader   or lover or enemy

even though   from you I have been absent

the spring unfolding   the imagination

shoots from the broken   clockwork of language

every woman dies   a thousand mediocre deaths

in a graceful imitation

of strange palms

and sea flowers   A sea flower

of a thousand colors   aquarium

pigmented   It is my violent

passion for sea flowers,

I want the entire

underwater palace

built of roaring sea flowers!

*

1. I enjoy high art but realism

swamps me.

2. The material world swamps me too.

3. I came to understand

the forms of realism,

the aesthetic phenomenon.

4. You take a random person from daily life.

5. You take their dependence

on their historical circumstances.

6. You make them

the subject.

7. You see, they operate

the modern.

Things happen . . . minutes, hours, days.

The order of life
coming from life itself.
"Back to life /
Back to reality."
It is sublime
and grotesque.
8. They make rich forms.

Something steady.
Less manic.
Something real
like a bell.

9. To what degree
are the subjects
taken seriously?

*

Or maybe built of something more maddening
more real   something steady   not my hands
but I can't tell   Inside this history
I'm unwell For example   when I broke you
and Craig up by inserting myself   into   your narrative
violent like my body   I created
the story   as a story of revenge
operatic and bloody   as any trauma
I hope I'm not creepy Molly   telling you
these things   my longing   so fractured
you and me inside   our spherical understandings
Mine philosophical   cut by theory and long
hours of study   as one would cut
a woman's form   from cold marble

Yours cut from   pragmatic understanding
          years in AA   the truths   you have memorized
recited like prayers   for survival which are also
          the weapons   one needs when left in the spring's
wilderness swirling   around us   Don't you see
               the emerald kayak
               and the femme fatale
who sleeps in it   Victorian
          long   frothy hair
          and the death drive
               flesh like the statement "I lost
a friend   in the sea garden"
The vortices of notes   staccato   vortex-like
          paradisiacal gold bell in a coffin
just in case I wake up   And the way
               darkness tunnels
inside a car on its way
to its pinpoint   destination
   No one tells you
the moon's going
          to be like this
No one So you just move
          towards it   That's all
the moon ever was
          Ding   Ding

*

[I was crying a lot] [I was also one of them] [I couldn't be excluded] [I wanted to opt out]
[I was a human shield] [I wanted to "get off the grid"] [I was crying a lot and it was embarrassing]
[I was one of the ones who couldn't "manage" my emotions] [In wife time, I was more like a wolf]
[I kept trying to deflect this truth] [Give me the fucking medicine, I said] [I got angry and lashed out]
[Give it to me right now, you fucking cunt] [I couldn't help it] [I knew that it was against the rules]

[The rules were simple: ignore intimacy] [Ignore the wet parts of the body] [Keep clicking do yoga
be younger work out be full of health] [Never go under under any circumstances] [Be unified] [Be
consistent] [Be controlled] [Never contort space with flesh] [Manage your house] [Manage your kids]
[Manage your student loans] [Manage to write poems] [Manage] [Manage]

    Wave of information after
        wave of information.
          It was a "we have found the plane at the
             bottom of the Indian Ocean" kind
              of wave. It was a "you're going to work
           from your grave" kind of wave.
        Wavelength of
          grave. Wavelength of hair
             engraved. Wave of the grass over
           the waves of the graves.

      *

"You have to own it," you said about life,
about buying a house in Tallahassee with a pool
  and my children swam in that pool
with your three gorgeous sisters.
  Kafka also had three gorgeous
sisters; they died in concentration camps.
 I don't know why I'm saying this
but in such a dying state
  there is no psychic relief since
the only way to protect against this
  ordinary history, these mundane
capitalist gestures is to layer the story
  as one descends through layers of cloud
over Orlando, pink and furious.

You made them macaroni and cheese
 which triggered my rage, made
me snap because I didn't want to be
   replaced as a mother or lover in this
world of substitution and empire.

Wherein the phenomenon of passion
                opens the door
                        to the nervous breakdown's form

Wherein passion
           disperses
                 the spirits

Wherein passion emerges as rage,
            paranoia, anorexia, melancholy,
                  or a combination of all of these things

Wherein passion
            confines
                 the real

Wherein passion pushes the limits
            of the real into the realm
                 of bodily displacement

Wherein we live within these capitalist
            parameters of known/
                  unknown values

Wherein there are boundaries fixed by money, property,
                 genitalia, geographical location,
                       race, education, and so on

Wherein ideology fills every conceivable
                space transforming the interior world of shame, guilt, deception, desire,
                into some new desire

      So, the only thing to do is to do
       whatever it takes: go crazy,
          pretend to go crazy,
      suicidal gestures from the doom palms.
      But what the subject doesn't know
      is the story of the substitute *is*
      the substitute so there is in fact
      a difference since wherever there
      is an impasse, a space of internal
      displacement that longs for just one
      moment of relief from the risk
      of loss, there is hope for something new.

      *

But I took you seriously   swimming beneath
    the icy sheet   of reality
since we are in the end on the same side of the patriarchy
    as you cut the hair   of the bourgeoisie
so pretty the sky   and even though you
    got over what I did to you
  You made macaroni and cheese   for Craig
and my kids   and dropped it off   at their house
  Later that night I went over   to Craig's house
and had sex with him and then ate the food you made
and after I left   sent you a picture of the food as proof
I had all the control You called me a bully messaged me
 "I don't understand   If Craig is so abusive why do you
leave your children with him and go out of town?"

Molly, time moves
even the worst stories   forward
    Months later you   had a new boyfriend
moved to Portland with him   and your dog
and how the story   was only the story
    due to the intervention   in the story
and how I claimed   I was vastly
    more intelligent   than you but
what I meant was, Dantesque, we could
    make a new intelligence   a new life
like pilgrims   of the contemporary   flaunting our
    spring light   like dresses   but this is not
something   one says   out loud unless
    fueled by the mad pursuit   of desire, rage, spite,
despair, the fire burning   months later when
    it extinguished no one   wants to go down
this unfortunate path   or scale its   terrible walls

    *

I'm a witch who lost all her powers,
 and in place of my powers, I got the coiled beauty
  of seashells and sleeping infants. The coiled
beauty of eardrums, and the sound wave
 of bells. The bells! This is the country of clouds.
    The molten body, the Floridian pinks,
     and centuries of sand dollars examining
the arcing waves. New territory
 of interiority and I'm in the middle of this.
  White like a negative belt.
I am an airless thing. When I get high, I get low.
    But I'm real and airless.

*

It was a time
of precarity. All kinds
of time. We were living
on scree.
Someone always there to like your dumb
dream or the dumb
things your kids say or the new swing set.

Be parking lot.
One more selfie
closer to Ross
Dress for Less.
Be friendly.
Dress like you're from Connecticut.
B+ / be surplus.
Sometimes B-. Collapse
the personality. Don't fuck away
my agony just to replace
it with more agony.
Be cunt? Be wet. Be kind.
Be Whole Foods orchids. Be pursuit.
Be benevolent. Pursuant.
Be communicable. Make claims.
Claim everything.
Then reverse it.

Poet be
like "like" or whatever. Poet be like list.
That's the body
electric. And it hums. It hums a
dumb electronic hum.

*

Then I stopped inside the fire   and inside
the fire there was a diner   and inside
    the diner my thoughts   were also
a fire   I will write   a feminist
    epic poem   about everything
no matter   how much   the gods
    kill me and the diner   became a book
of poetry regardless   of my will I can't
    hijack January February March April May
Star Wars cereal   and the diner's eggs
    cold   on the cold counter where
the cold waitress   adds some cold black
    mascara to   her cold checkered
doom apron right then
    and there   I wanted to sing this song:

If it could   snow in Orlando
    If the waitress   could look out the window
and see the snow   If she had dreams of snow
    that materialized   as the backdrop
to the diner   If she   was dreaming
    the dreams   of snow piling on
like characters whose   narratives blur
    snow   in Orlando the chandelier dream
of a spring snow   the snows of the now
    and the sepia snows   of nostalgia
the howling snows   of the future
    and the equally   horrid snows of the no
future all of this snow   that signifies we are
    all new and the   sorrow-filled winter Orlando snow
that says   we were never new and why
    would you believe   we were in the first place?
If she could look sadly   at the snow

that says these   things to you
and makes you feel   these things
     you did   not feel before   as I did not
and as   all the characters   did not feel
     since this is   the green imagery of what
can exist   what can be imagined

                    *

We call this utopia   we call
     this some   paradisiacal knowledge
but you have   to see the pomegranates
     you have to trust   it exists
you have   to imagine it which doesn't
     come to everyone   (the shade, figure and form)
In other words   the living and dead
     so difficult to see   since we
are at opposite ends   of the story you
   being the subject   (the living)   and I being
the object (the dead)   and therefore
     I am at your mercy though I am   the one
to construct your feelings   inside the plot
     of feeling   constructed where   it is snowing
and the plot fills   with so much snow
     it can no longer be   a grave and thus
you shall   never die nor I   as we are
     the ones saved   from the confines   of the story
because we were put   there by the maker
     which is   the intelligence   of me and you
put together   combined as it were
     snow and snow   we become
spring water   even if   that was never

the intent   as I say these   things to you
and the waitress   pours your coffee
     to warm you   as I warm you

If she is as beautiful   as the snow
     we are looking at together right here
in this blue box   of spring patterned
     like everything   like meaning itself
If she could   ride time
     patterned like snow   through Orlando
If we could just   get a glimpse
     into her suffering   and the snow could
signify   our understanding
     of her psychology   which is complicated
yet serene If we could know   through snow
     I hear so much   I want to know
When I get low   I get high   like literature
     where it is snowing violently   for a moment
and then the snow eases up and   our waitress
     is staring at the snow   longingly like a dog
wearing a   silly red ribbon around
     his neck   inside a house
inside a   poem   inside the diner
     inside the fire   one day destroys
another day
          moves onward
into the sun
          glistens
and we walk
          out of the sun
turns so easily
          into a brochure

I find on a desk
        at my university
stare at the pages
        burning the edges with
 the memory of my mother
        who hated me
feeling lost   alone   ashamed
    having never been   a daughter but always
an object   or prostitute   for her boyfriend
   which no longer   feels shameful but factual
9/12/98   You have   to help me   I'm crazy
    I just can't help   feeling fucking crazy
and then BAM   I decide   I should just retract
    into this shell of mine   I'm fucking sick
I want   Joe to call   Freud   said containing
    the inside   on the inside   makes a person sane
Well then what   does that make me?
    Come on   open your gates   I'm hungry
I'm bored I'm split   in half   Why do I always
    choose to be the model   the beautiful model
I'm living in some   hallucinatory hiatus
    A love charm   demons

            *

[Be collected] [Tell yourself there is no harm done] [Be collected] [But what about the precarious
spectacle of this wreck?] [See the papier-mâché sculpture of the supermax prison my kids made?]
[See your mouth frozen inside the paperweight?] [Some compressed compassion breaks the surface]
[The state where they spy on you or copy you] [Copy and spy] [Copy and spy trap] [A spike in the
weather says I am spring] [Then the barometric drop] [Then dancing] [Then the girl who wore the
tube top who was immediately gang-raped by the social sphere]

            *

Baudelaire   says all love   is prostitution
     which I read   as despair   in my heart
laid bare   and mine   right here
     barely   a diary   the question
is how once   prostituted   to the sun
     moon to   the mother's boyfriend
does one return   to the source   the little
     girl waiting   at the window   for night
to turn   into a white car   not demonic yet
     to bring forth the spring   of perhaps not innocence
but the revolving grass   I see you
     I acknowledge you   despair freeing itself
from the confines   of its twisted logic
     so as to move towards   a new consciousness
and push the parameters   of the real
     past the walls   of trauma as Chris said
"it's the most conservative   thing we do
     go back   to what we know   like dogs"
and still the heart   now a hole   in the ground
     to bury the poem   or the brochure   a grave
you won't   be a good parent   voices say   you will fail
     as I have failed   your faculties   will fail
you will stay   in this box   I command you
     inside   the fire   in the diner   in Orlando

*

Of all the trees, the oak
     is the most powerful
of bells and bees. Heartbreakingly
     you reverberate lily-shaped
  like a child with heavy eyelashes,
     filling in a coloring book
of blizzards and bells.

Pacts made with Satan
    are signed in musical notes,
 snow and bees that stab,
   you see. One drop
of menstrual blood inside a glass bee
    gives bad dreams
but can mean anything.

An oak planted at a crossroads
   has healing powers. Wren-like women
    cause fruit to fall from trees.
   A glance from one
   of them will kill
 a swarm of crystals and bells.

The bells! The bells!
Semitone above, semitone below, a bow arcs
    out in the blue wind of roaring
dresses, watery bell-shaped
  notes fluttering, like the streaming
sun inside forms of snow so single-mindedly
   driven by these springtime cells—
    walking to the farmer's market,
    they dangle from my frost-like body,
     they are gold chains, I feel them dwindle,
   devalue, so call me crystalline
    and I will never dread
   the mechanized world of my head.

    *

Molly, you're the empress
      of all things, aquamarine—impressionist interpretation
     of something wet, serene in the jellyfish
    blue of the afternoon,
   cylindrical, dock pilings, your long, sad personal history
held up like a white flag I made up. I had what
  I had, fig perfume unravelled, rivulets
 of it collecting in the corner like wallflowers
who want to dance but can't, like ghosts
            who live where darkness alternates
    the current of nothing
        embedded in a future
   like seduction is to prayer
     an analogy so rare
   the object of desire
     a text, the context
  a bunch of neurons
     Beluga! Ice tulips!
Atlantis! Panchaea!
     Island where you cannot
bury the dead
   placed against
the conditions of possibility
    frankincense oozing
forth like tears
    the maker drinks
some coffee
   so lonely life is
in the interstitial surplus
    hot Florida pavement
I get in my car
   to pick up
my kids *vroom vroom*

*

Prostitution need not   take the literal form
     For example, this brochure   detailing the benefits
of becoming   a Florida Child   Protective
     Services Officer $39,934 a year
9 days off   feeling lost and alone
     on my way home   stopped at a South Georgia
gas station   bought Skittles
     Diet Coke   a bag of peaches and a man
slammed his car door said, "Damn, woman,
     you're fuckin' beautiful, you know that?
Do you know what I do all day? I take these
        poor fuckin' kids from
            their poor fuckin'
            families and put
them in foster care. You have to know
     how some parents
treat their children like animals or worse.
           I saw a toddler chained
in a backyard," and lit a cigarette,
        drove down the highway towards Florida
           and swept away by the smell of peach
     lush trees   jays
      the upper air fluttering there's
      no in-between layers
     of these cold clouds
combine above   the desk classroom
 university gas station
     the gates   of the sun
like a lioness I am some-
    thing more Leo

to make the story

of pain longer   more entwined

than the Edda or the poem   is sitting

on some grassy knoll

where predictable

outbursts of rain denote

the chaotic summer

of the last poem   and the new buds

of this one like a dress

once white with death

dyed a beautiful purple   the purple

of the aristocratic spring

which is the soul

untarnished   a choir   and the rains

of delight   fall on the purple dress

no need to confess   Oh greenest

branch, hail! forged

in the fading of memory

and you can sit   inside the shade

that fills   all technologically driven affect

with water   and how

this affect rots the dizzying trees

then   all the dissolved   jays leave

[Goodbye, honey!] [Nighty night, Malaysia 370!] [Hello, Whitman!] [In the waves, there were our bodies in waves and some were waving noooooo and some were waving goodbyeeeeee and some were waving hellooooo] [Second-wave medieval state] [All peasants get swallowed into the underworld and Orfeo plays] [his wooden lute] [And the queen is saved] [And then everyone sees Orfeo was really the king] [though dressed like a pauper] [And when we take off our dresses] [we will still be slaves] [And when they make our skin digits] [we will still be slaves]

*

A lioness pendant to greet the new
    hierarchy. *Aha!* Now that lioness becomes
the sincerity of a colorless collapse, how one
 we grow, corpse,
    your cool avenues avow anew.

On the face of it,
    but there is no face. She threw a couple
of coral beads in the mix of gold chain
    but I knew they were orange
plastic, arranged diplomatically just
    like relief or water
        because she hates me.

      *

      [And when they cure our cancers, we will still be slaves] [And when they make us healthier again, we will still be slaves]

      *

      "I love my family," I said.
      "You, me, Charlotte."
        Ezekiel   climbed into my bed
   in the morning said,
       "Every man for himself."
I said,   "Where did you hear this?"
    "A Geico commercial," and then he said,
"I wish upon a star for   the end of money,"
    and I said, "Me and you
      here this is the end
of money   Don't you see that?"
      The end of money is a well of affection

a tenderness a comet stirs the plants
O blood of mine   as effusive   as I am all days
destroying all the other days.

[And when they say, "Don't write poems with stories or emotions," we will still be slaves] [And when they say make some conceptual art in five minutes that everyone talks about] [we will still be slaves] [And when we read the stories that we have been told we shouldn't write] [then we will begin to not be slaves] [And when we begin to make our stories real] [then we will start to not be slaves]

*

You must know this   is a mess   an affective bargain
      a fantasy of form   my friend Alex
asked "but who is Molly"   my friend Matthew asked
      "but who is Orlando"   my friend Abe asked
"but who is Chris"   my friend Brandi said
      "I don't understand this"   I said "I don't know
them yet   They are only a means   to keep
      living   or wave of flourishing subjects"

*

It might be thrilling to pretend
      that instead of living   at the end of empire
we are at the beginning of it   and we can
      dip our bodies   into the real   waterfalls
of life   align them   in our minds
      with the fake waterfalls   of the future
so that two versions   of reality can sing
      one ideological   and one pure image
against each other   harmony and melody
      rise and fall   bloom superimposed
on flowers that   when pressed   make

the cheeks flush red with reproductions
not worse waterfalls   the resurrection
    chlorinated and designed   by a political
economy that falters   eats up the bodies
    of the poor   and churns out water
as a cheap   Niagara Falls–like alienation
    the limits of the working day   once thought
to be the limits   of the body   or Mercury
    The old poets begged   for the prison doors
to fly open   the new poets beg for
    them   to slam shut

                *

        I can see us now   two bodies constellated
    inside a revolving utopia   two fields of flesh
            made possible   through fantasy
    We become 1970s tick   tock bell-bottoms
            slinging our vampiric flesh   against anything
    that will take us back   to our longing
back to the primeval forest   of jaguar-shaped
            irises or a filter for   the Ivy League
        technology of the dollhouse
        of the dollhouse
            of the dollhouse of feeling
                    and money
space of comfort
            and long-lost secrets
    so that the mistress
            of the game decodes
        the frost   as the heart and will
        break in increments

and the sun feeds on and on
and on and on and on
and there is no past
like this   Some memory
of being in a pine forest
collecting fossils
with Ezekiel and Charlotte
under the garbage bag
of the sun or Jana Watson
in her molten, coral-colored dress
on the cover of the *Bay Eagle*, high school
newspaper, singers holding hands
as if they know   the future is just a template they must follow
Don't cry, Molly,   Don't cry, Jana
with the perfect skin, murdered by Nietzsche,
Disney, the Bible, Robert Frost,
or the humid death wind

*

Few people would dare kill a wren.
The cauldron of love
is deep, contains personal
and political failures,
war, self-torture,
child abuse, the chromatic
scale, oh song down
the sundown waters.

He said it took five months
to recover, that he was in a wheelchair
and lived with his mother. Wrens

were abundant in the eaves but one day
they disappeared. The day
his broken leg healed,
the house fell like trees.

*3/2/2002 Smoked, drank a lot last night,
heart was just pounding, anxiety, or just
my body? Psychiatrists here make $250/hour,
I make $16. Andrew woke up
in the middle of the night
and wanted to fuck. Ginger 414-743-6476
Why are you so enraptured by my face?*

*8/17/1998 We are going to Italy tomorrow. I'm so
excited. We walked to the Mer de Glace glacier (this a.m.)
and it started storming. It was kind of scary to see the storm
from the top of the mountain. My poetry professor says
you can't write the words "I love you" in a poem anymore.
I want to go to every country in Europe and pick all the flowers
and ride all the trains. The problem is that the sky doesn't
know me anymore—I just want you to let me throw
my clouds around you and pray. Insanity, to the sane,
seems so pointless.*

That's the problem with the archive, Sandra. It doesn't
actually say anything. It doesn't matter if your mother's
boyfriend tried to fuck you or dyed your hair red in his apartment
in Playa del Rey. It doesn't matter if he made you suck
his dick in his bathroom as a kid. The archive is as bad
as the bourgeoisie. Even yours. All I see is red light and vomit.
Don't you see how it lies? Don't you see how this is part
of the violence? You just want tulips, roses, dandelions.
There are no clues in the lines. Your talk about Italy,
flowers, and the bloom of trains.

*

In April, bells mean towers
          mean lightning means
     wrens means death omen
          means dolphins
          have a weakness for human
          singing means
          carrying Orlando
          to the afterlife
     means rigid structures
          to guide the dead day means
     the sheen of water means
     the Fahrenheit air
          glistening means
the sudden disappearance
     of a nest means
          your survival is guaranteed.

*

Police brutality makes me want to starve
     myself to death and loneliness
          sucks   Grapes   palms
and pomegranates do not grow
     here anymore and we don't
     understand finance capital since we are all
plaintiffs and you can't   live up to the fantasy
     of myself I've laid on the table
          for you   So why praise
the elaborate song patterns   of the comatose lyric
     or walk in the morgue of
          conceptual poetry   ID the body
     "What's up, Daddy?"   When the plants

                    are sparkling with that glorious   toxic glow
                          chilly   fancy financial   fluttering   vines
            and nosy dolphins are   interfering with commerce
                    and the waterline   but happily
            they splash in the hot   Gulf of trash
Their pods so unfree   poison me

                    *

Dragging the real
        into the poem
from the real
        of the open form
until it transforms
        into a vocabulary
        rich and true,
white-cap sea dealt deathly
        structured of a pearl,
"I just feel this pain,"
        some vision so frail
        you might fail to
think it's real

The day Craig dragged me around
 our bedroom by the neck was the day
something   broke   the cadence
        is the nature of this confinement
boxes, cells, the text growing
        out of these boundaries

In medieval miniatures, gems
        and flowers are considered beautiful

Circles are beautiful
 The brilliance of simple
       colors and light
Lux is light itself   *Lumen*
 is light that travels through space
       Splendor is the light of luminous bodies
which I take to be the light of ideas or death

When people say, "I'm so sorry that happened to you,"
       I feel a corporate terror

       *

Locked in the beauty of the pearl,
far from frail, a mellow rain flows
  over Orlando
Orlando, place of raw material, place of affect,
  place of this lush box, the pulse so lush
   it makes the live version of history
       stream before you like tears

       1. Imagines snakes are after her with obscene intentions.
       2. Does not know her name.
       3. Thinks herself to be the Virgin Mary.
       4. This woman is a raving maniac who can give no account of herself.
       5. She is naked.
       6. If you ask her what is the matter with her she cries like a child and asks to be taken away
              from that man (her imagined enemy).
       7. She is naked.

       *

Rose-tinted photo of me, Sandra Simonds, walking toward the garden
     Red shoe half off
Rose-tinted photo of me, Sandra Simonds, moving toward the eggplant
Strawberries, the rotten shed
that I rent, that isn't mine, that will never be mine
Moving ever toward everything that isn't mine
          Except the subject

Rose-tinted baby holding the trowel
who looks not toward me
but toward some distant bird beyond
the photographer
The sky pink like a seizure
Eruption of data
The foaming present forming layers
and layers of figures in waves
The lair the lumber the lugging
     Still lugging shreds of the intimate

          *

  "Is Pippi Spanish?"
"No, from Sweden," I tell Ezekiel.
    "Where's that?" "North of here.
Near where Loki comes from."

It's the end
     of the world and a gigantic wolf
is going to swallow
     the coagulated sun whole.
Myth, wish-fulfillment. He broke
  the strongest chains ever built.

He was strong.
He won.
I'm not strong.
I don't win.

Pippi Longstocking is strong too.
And smart.

Sit with me, little one,
   inside this mansion of June
   hieroglyphics, inside
the belle lettres of fluttering
    paper-doll tomorrows,

and mourn
   how we never lived.

      *

Psychoanalysis and weeping, sublimated sexual
  energy dispersed over gym equipment mixed
           with garden-variety capitalist alienation—
crazed mom, glittering dick, electronic
supermoon, flat on the floor, gratified,
    dignity reduced, struck a nerve,
  drug-veined and whining.
  Why are you whining?
   I am thy garden.
    And the fallen tree.
   I am thy Minecraft.
    And the fallen tree.
    I am thy opus

and opium. And the fallen tree.
I am thy dignitary.
And the fallen tree.
I am thy thee.
And the fallen tree.
I weep for
you thee thy thee.
La di da di di.
And the fallen tree.

O power yet to come.
O future might.
O vigor.
The impending future loves
your fecundity.
O future haste.
Enough to bloom.

When's life going to start?

*

Swaggering like rain like rain like rain
and swaggering the day the day the day
and swaggering it raineth all day all day
and swaggering I claimed I claimed
I claimed And swaggering the dog the dog the dog
And swaggering anew anew anew and swaggering
for you for you for you and swaggering I felt
I felt I felt and swaggering at night in spite in spite
And swaggering inside I died I died

*

Fanny Kaplan shot Lenin and I'm in this box, destitute of light,
    desperate. Arson is a lilac
perfume, suck in the arsenic flame, next door the neighbors
  are drunk fighting
  about drunk fighting and the status of women
in society, "Fuck, Jean. You ain't my mama, you're
my woman," the gates of hell
    roaring like power, rat poison
makes you swim faster and faster, and I don't care
  how a person ought to be, blood thinning, Molly,
    I care how a person
        should live.

*

The forest of reality is the end of song.
    The bourgeois families
are headed toward their
      picnics and meadows. Ruin
  all night long, the roses
and flags drape the dead man,
  something splendid creeps into the darkness,
  darkness like wet thigh
  on wet thigh, and at the base
of the valley, it's the end of everything,
      mimetic, divine,
        driven like a nail
      into the dread of the world.

*

All master narratives of the mind in a rowboat and the rowboat as beautiful as the swamp
glowing, the dungeon state lily pads unfolding like riddles of water, the Plasticine
heads of amphibians, speckled skin of religious fervor, and the razor-blade weeds.

All master narratives of the body in a rowboat at the bottom of the swamp that has no hands.

All master narratives of the spirit in the rowboat sky reflecting the infant swamp, clouds of filth, soil
knotted like tupelos and toppled alphabets.

All master narratives of the skin in a rowboat inside a pine coffin of swamp water.

All master narratives of thinking like a woman who says, "I chose inappropriate relationships."

All master narratives of dramatic structure in the soggy swamp, against the humid flags beating the
wind.

All master narratives of mythology like my son saying, "And then he turned into a very big wolf."

"I think he was very sad."

"He has feelings too, you know."

"I think he was sad because he got trapped inside the doors."

"Oh my god, there are different Fenrirs."

"Loki's Fenrir met a different Fenrir."

"Are wolves part of the cat family?"

"Hey, look up on your phone if they can change forms because these guys look different from the real Fenrir."

"See that white picture where he's up on top? He turns huge and tries to eat the sun."

"Oh, that's a tough Fenrir."

"I think he obeys the serpent."

"Now that's sad Fenrir."

"Or maybe Loki turns into the serpent."

"Oh, Loki, are you a master of evil?"

"I think they can change forms."

ACKNOWLEDGMENTS

Parts of this book have appeared in *Poetry*, *Granta*, *Verse*, *Brooklyn Rail*, *Bennington Review, Puerto del Sol*, and *Conduit*. Thank you to the editors of these publications for including earlier drafts of my work in these journals.

Deep gratitude to Matthew Zapruder whose editorial guidance and support of this book, from the very beginning, have been invaluable; Heidi Broadhead and everyone at Wave for their careful editorial attention to the book; Abraham Smith, Carmen Giménez Smith, Shanna Compton, Dyan Neary, and Alexander Papanicolopoulos for their friendship and support.

Some phrases in the book are taken from Lauren Berlant, Umberto Eco, Erich Auerbach, and Walter Benjamin.

This book is for my sister.